Let's Have a Bake Sale

Calculating Profit and Unit Cost

Frances E. Ruffin

PowerMath™

The Rosen Publishing Group's
PowerKids Press™
New York

Published in 2004 by The Rosen Publishing Group, Inc.
29 East 21st Street, New York, NY 10010

Book Design: Haley Wilson

Photo Credits: Cover © Kindra Clineff/Index Stock; p. 4 (photos of dogs and cats) © PhotoDisc; all other
interior photos by Maura B. McConnell.

Library of Congress Cataloging-in-Publication Data

Ruffin, Frances E.
  Let's have a bake sale : calculating profit and unit cost / Frances E.
Ruffin.
      p. cm. — (PowerMath)
Includes index.
Summary: Explains how to make a profit at a small business venture, such
as a bake sale, focusing on how to determine the unit cost of an item in
order that a profit can be made.
  ISBN 0-8239-8970-4 (Library binding)
  ISBN 0-8239-8893-7 (Paperback)
  6-pack ISBN: 0-8239-7421-9
  1. Business mathematics—Juvenile literature. 2. Small
business—Juvenile literature. 3. Problem solving—Juvenile literature.
[1. Moneymaking projects. 2. Profit. 3. Business mathematics.] I.
Title. II. Series.
  HF5691 .R867 2004
  658'.041—dc21
                              2002155652 2002154484

Manufactured in the United States of America

Contents

Bake Sale Profits

Our class decided to have a bake sale to earn money for the **animal shelter** in our town. We hoped to earn $125.00 for the shelter.

To figure out how much to charge for each **item** at the bake sale, we first had to figure out how much it cost to make or buy each item. Then we had to sell each item for more than the amount we paid for it. The difference between what we paid for the item and what we sold it for is called a **profit**. The total profit we made on the bake sale was money we could give to the animal shelter.

There are many other ways that we could have raised money for the animal shelter. We could have held a car wash or sold candy. These are all ways to earn money and make a profit.

To find out how much 1 donut cost, we divided $3.00 (the cost for 1 box) by 12 (the number of donuts in 1 box).
The cost of 1 donut was $0.25.

$$\begin{array}{r} \$0.25 \\ 12\overline{\smash)\$3.00} \\ -24 \\ \hline 60 \\ -60 \\ \hline 0 \end{array}$$

Donuts for Dollars

Our class set a **goal** to earn $50.00 for the animal shelter by selling donuts. We decided to buy the donuts at the store. We bought 10 boxes of donuts for a total of $30.00. Each box had 12 donuts, so there were 120 donuts altogether. How much did each donut cost?

First, we figured out what 1 box of donuts cost. Look at the box on this page to see what we found.

To find out how much 1 donut cost, we divided the cost of 1 box of donuts ($3.00) by the number of donuts in the box (12). The cost of 1 donut was $0.25. Look at the box on page 6 to see how we did the math!

To find out what 1 box of donuts cost, we divided the total price we paid for all the boxes ($30.00) by the number of boxes we bought (10). **The cost of 1 box of donuts was $3.00.**	$$\begin{array}{r} \$3.00 \\ 10\overline{)\$30.00} \\ -30 \\ \hline 0 \end{array}$$

Our class made a total of $84.00 by selling all the donuts.

$$
\begin{array}{r}
^1120 \\
\times \$0.70 \\
\hline
000 \\
840 \\
\hline
\$84.00
\end{array}
$$

donuts
per donut

from sale of
120 donuts

8

Selling All the Donuts

We decided to sell the donuts for $0.70 each. At the bake sale, we sold all the donuts. How much money did we have after selling all the donuts? Look at the box on page 8 to find the answer.

We can figure out the profit we made by subtracting the amount that it cost to buy the donuts at the store from the total amount the donuts sold for at the bake sale. If you look at the box on this page, you'll see that our class made a profit of $54.00 from the sale of the donuts.

Our class made a profit of $54.00 from the donut sale. That is $4.00 more than our goal of $50.00!

$84.00	from sale of 120 donuts
−30.00	to buy donuts at the store
$54.00	profit for the animal shelter

The total cost of the supplies to make lemonade was $15.00.

$$\begin{array}{r} \$11.00 \\ 1.00 \\ +\ \ 3.00 \\ \hline \$15.00 \end{array}$$

It cost $0.30 per cup to make 50 cups of lemonade.

$$\begin{array}{r} \$0.30 \\ 50\overline{)\$15.00} \\ -150 \\ \hline 00 \end{array}$$

Making Lemonade

Our class also decided to sell lemonade at the bake sale. We found a **recipe** that made 50 cups of lemonade. We needed to buy 20 lemons for $11.00, 5 cups of sugar for $1.00, and 50 paper cups for $3.00. What was the total cost to buy the supplies we needed? We added the prices of the 3 items together to find out. Look at the box on page 10 to see how we did the math!

To find out what each cup of lemonade cost us, we divided our total **expenses** by the number of cups. We found that each cup of lemonade cost $0.30 to make, including the cost of the paper cup.

When we figured out the cost of making lemonade, we remembered to include the paper cups we would have to buy. The paper cups were part of our expenses, along with the lemons and sugar.

We made a total of $40.00 by selling all the lemonade.

$$\begin{array}{r} \overset{4}{\$0.80} \\ \times\ \ 50 \\ \hline 000 \\ 400\ \ \ \\ \hline \$40.00 \end{array}$$

per cup of lemonade

cups of lemonade

from sale of 50 cups of lemonade

12

Lemonade for Sale!

Our class decided to sell each cup of lemonade for $0.80. We sold all 50 cups of lemonade. We wanted to figure out how much money we had after we sold all the lemonade. Look at the box on page 12 to see how we figured out how much money we made by selling 50 cups of lemonade for $0.80 per cup.

We can figure out the profit our class made from selling the lemonade by subtracting our expenses from the total amount we made by selling the lemonade. If you look at the box on this page, you'll see that we made a $25.00 profit for the animal shelter by selling lemonade.

Our class made a profit of $25.00 from the lemonade sale.	$40.00 from sale of 50 cups of lemonade −15.00 to buy all the supplies to make lemonade $25.00 profit for the animal shelter

2 lemon pies
3 blueberry pies
7 cherry pies
+10 apple pies
_____
22 pies

It cost us
$66.00 to
buy 22 pies.

$3.00 per pie
x 22 pies
_____
600
600
_____
$66.00 to buy 22 pies

Pies for Profit

Our class thought that pies would be a good thing to sell at the bake sale. Every person in the class brought 1 pie to the bake sale. Each pie cost $3.00 to buy at the store. There were 2 lemon pies, 3 blueberry pies, 7 cherry pies, and 10 apple pies. How much did it cost to buy all the pies?

To find out, we first added up the number of pies. There were 22 pies altogether. Then we multiplied the total number of pies by the amount each pie cost ($3.00). It cost us $66.00 to buy 22 pies at the store. Look at the box on page 14 to see how we figured this out.

If the 22 pies had cost $88.00 altogether, what would have been the cost of 1 pie? Divide $88.00 by 22 to find the answer.

1 pie would have cost $4.00.

$$\begin{array}{r} \$4.00 \\ 22\overline{)\$88.00} \\ -88 \\ \hline 000 \end{array}$$

PIE SALE
$5.00 a PIE

Our class made a total of $110.00 by selling all the pies.

$5.00 per pie
x 22 pies sold
1000
1000
$110.00 from the sale of 22 pies

So Many Pies!

Our class decided we would sell each pie at the bake sale for $5.00. We sold all 22 pies! To find out how much money we had after all the pies were sold, we multiplied the price of each pie ($5.00) by the number of pies sold (22). To see how we did the math, look at the box on page 16.

Then we wanted to find out how much profit we made on the sale of the pies. We subtracted the original cost of all the pies from the total amount that all the pies sold for at the bake sale. Look at the box on this page to see how we figured it out. You can see that our class made a profit of $44.00 to give to the animal shelter!

Our class made a profit of $44.00 from the pie sale.	$\overset{0\ 10\ 1}{\$110.00}$ from sale of 22 pies
	$-\ 66.00$ to buy 22 pies at the store
	$\$44.00$ profit for the animal shelter

Brownie mix: 6 boxes of brownie mix
               x $2.00 per box = $12.00

Eggs: 1 dozen (12) eggs cost $1.50

Vegetable oil: 1 bottle cost $1.50

$12.00 for brownie mix
  1.50 for a dozen eggs
÷ 1.50 for 1 bottle of oil
$15.00 to make 60 brownies

The Cost of Brownies

Our class wanted to earn $25.00 for the animal shelter by selling brownies. We decided to make 60 brownies for the bake sale. Since 1 box of brownie mix makes 10 brownies, we had to buy 6 boxes of brownie mix. We also needed to buy a dozen (12) eggs and a bottle of vegetable oil to add to the brownie mix.

We added the cost of all the ingredients together. It cost $15.00 to make 60 brownies. To see how we figured this out, look at the box on page 18.

Then we needed to figure out what it cost to make 1 brownie. Look at the box on this page to find our answer.

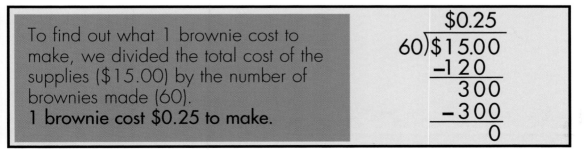

To find out what 1 brownie cost to make, we divided the total cost of the supplies ($15.00) by the number of brownies made (60).
1 brownie cost $0.25 to make.

$$\begin{array}{r} \$0.25 \\ 60\overline{)\$15.00} \\ -120 \\ \hline 300 \\ -300 \\ \hline 0 \end{array}$$

Brownie Sale
75¢ per Brownie

Our class made a total of $45.00 by selling 60 brownies.

$$
\begin{array}{r}
\overset{4\ \ 3}{\$0.75} \text{ per brownie} \\
\times\ \underline{\quad 60\ } \text{ brownies sold} \\
000 \\
450\quad \\
\hline
\$45.00
\end{array}
$$

total made selling brownies

Everyone Loves Brownies

Our class decided to sell the brownies for $0.75 each at the bake sale. We sold all 60 brownies! When we multiplied the price for each brownie by the number of brownies, we figured out that we had made a total of $45.00 from the sale of the brownies. Look at the box on page 20 to see how we did the math!

By subtracting what it cost us to make the brownies from the total amount the brownies sold for, our class discovered that we had made a profit of $30.00 to give to the animal shelter. Look at the box on this page to see how we figured it out.

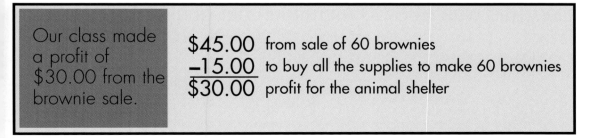

Our class made a profit of $30.00 from the brownie sale.

$$\begin{array}{ll} \$45.00 & \text{from sale of 60 brownies} \\ -15.00 & \text{to buy all the supplies to make 60 brownies} \\ \hline \$30.00 & \text{profit for the animal shelter} \end{array}$$

A Successful Bake Sale

We added up the profits we made at the bake sale. We sold donuts for a profit of $54.00. We sold lemonade for a profit of $25.00. We sold pies for a profit of $44.00. We sold brownies for a profit of $30.00. What was the total profit we made to give to the animal shelter?

$54.00 profit from donut sale
25.00 profit from lemonade sale
44.00 profit from pie sale
+ 30.00 profit from brownie sale
$153.00 total profit from all sales

When we added all the profits together, we found that our class raised a total of $153.00 to give to the animal shelter. This was $28.00 more than our goal of $125.00. Our bake sale was a huge success!

Glossary

animal shelter (AN-uh-muhl SHEL-tuhr) A place that protects lost animals from weather and danger.

expense (ihk-SPENS) Money spent for something.

goal (GOHL) A purpose. Something to aim for. The school's goal was to raise $125.00 for the animal shelter.

item (I-tuhm) A single thing. One thing on a list.

profit (PRAH-fuht) The money a company or group of people makes after all its bills are paid.

recipe (REH-suh-pea) A list of directions for making something to eat or drink.

Index